I Was Born, Now What?

I Was Born, Now What?
A GUIDE TO SURVIVING TEENHOOD AND LIFE BEYOND

Be prepared for the day when you get the boot!

Jan Mendoza

Far West Publishing

I Was Born, Now What © 2009 Jan Mendoza

ISBN 9780982605004

Far West Publishing

All rights reserved. No part of this publication may be reproduced, stored in a retrieval system, or transmitted in any form or by any means, electronic, mechanical, recording or otherwise without the prior written permission of Jan Mendoza.

Manufactured in the United States of America.

Contents of this book are solely based on the opinions and experiences of the author. The author is not an attorney nor a medical professional. It is highly recommended to seek medical, legal and other professional advice from licensed professionals when embarking on any situations mentioned in this book.

Dedicated to

My husband Alex,
my family
and the rest of my dear friends

They all encouraged me and put up with my dream chasing.

Table of Contents

Part One
Boot Camp	7
High School	15
The School Work	16
Art of Learning	20
Learning Disorders	27
Teachers	29
Social/Ego	43

Part Two
Build your Boat	54
Licensed to Drive	55
Working	62
Your Health	65
Preparing for the Boot	79
Learn to Cook	80
Learn your Car	81
Learn your Finances	83

Part Three
Emancipation	85
College	87
Trade School	92
Military	95
Get a Job	104
Moving Out	105
Set Sail	107
Setting Goals	109
Bon Voyage	110
Quiz Answer Key	112

Introduction

From Birth to the Boot

So who asks to be born anyway? I used to ask this all the time when things were going terribly wrong. I was told that I was this little angel floating around up in heaven waiting my turn to come down to earth. Umm.....I don't remember any of that! So however we got here, we are here and I guess we need to make the best of it, right? Right!

For some of you, your conception was well thought out. Somebody thought that having a little bundle of joy around the house would be the most fantastic thing in the world.

For a lot of you, your arrival was a big surprise. I was one of those big "SURPRISE" babies.

As a child you didn't have a care in the world. You played, slept, watched TV, played, ate, slept, played games on the computer, slept, ate and played some more.

Life was fantastic! Then something horrible happens along the way. You grow up and get the boot. Now what?

If only a glimpse into life's journey was shown to me before I got the boot. I wasn't prepared for relationships, dealing with psycho bosses, finding and keeping a job, checking the oil in my car and maintaining a bank account among many other things.

I've spent my whole life trying to figure out the "Now What." If you were to ask me what my dream was while I was growing up, I would have told you professional singer. Now my dream is to get as much as I can accomplished before I die. In 2009 I turned 50 and have accomplished many things on my "to do" list, including my original dream of being a professional musician.

Believe me, the first 50 years have been a crazy ride with loads of ups and downs. I've experienced heartache and joy with every single one of my endeavors and there are some things that I wish I could do over. But, with no do-overs in life, I keep plugging along to get to the next thing on my list. I strive to be the queen of reinvention.

I've always liked the saying, "You are the captain of your own ship." You can either sail it out to peaceful happy waters, or you can run it up onto the rocks, gouge all kinds of holes in the hull and sink, it's your choice. You might hit a sandbar once in a while as you try and captain your ship, but like any good captain or pilot, you can work to get your ship unstuck and back out to sea.

I'm writing this "Captain's Manual" to help you get prepared for your journey on the sea of life. The waters can get rough out there but if you are a well trained captain, you will be able to handle any storm that comes your way.

As the captain of my own ship, I went on many adventures and traveled many oceans. I was determined to sail many waters and accomplish every goal I set out to do.

Here is a list of some of the things on my "To Do" list as I captained my ship:

- A forest firefighter (I was one of the first women to work for the California Department of Forestry.)
- Professional rock singer
- Radio DJ on country and rock stations
- Airborne traffic reporter. (I reported the traffic from the backseat of an airplane.)
- Paralegal (I went back to college at age 32 and opened my own paralegal business.)
- Co-producer of a burlesque production and owner of a talent agency
- Rodeo trick rider, (this is something I started in my 40s and I filmed my own documentary on trick riding. The DVD is sold around the world.)
- Horse trainer
- Jewelry maker (I have my own line of handmade jewelry.)
- Artist
- Author
- Filmmaker (I produce my own music videos.)

Along the way, I had to pay the bills and keep a roof over my head. Here are a few of the positions I held while working on my "To Do" list:

Unicom Operator (I told small airplanes on what runway to land) – secretary – medical biller – media spokesperson for the State of California – public relations – sales executive with Fortune 500 companies as clients – house cleaner – dental lab assistant – teacher's aid – waitress – house painter – retail/grocery clerk and bartender. I've also sold Mary Kay, Avon, Herbalife and other multi-level marketing company products.

If you are using the excuse that you don't have time to chase your dreams, think again. I accomplished my "To Do" list as a single mom while working full-time jobs.

When we are born, we grow up and then what?
Well future ship Captain here is your instruction manual!

Happy Sailing!

Part One

Boot Camp – Survival Training

It's War!

Before you can get promoted to Captain you must first go through boot camp. So, listen up Cadet Sailor! Do you pay rent? Do you pay the light, water and garbage bill? Do you pay for your own groceries? No? What's that, you're not an adult? I CAN'T HEAR YOU! You still live at home? What's that? You say that your mom, dad or someone else does all that stuff? Wow! You are very lucky Cadet Sailor!

Until you are legally considered an adult, there are adults in your life that are financially and legally responsible for your physical, financial and legal well-being. This is a fact and the law. In most states, you are considered an adult when you turn 18. In Alabama and Nebraska the legal adult age is 19 and in Mississippi it's 21. Until you reach the legal age of adulthood or are legally emancipated at a younger age, you really don't have much to say about anything. You will have some sort of legal guardian in your life until you reach that magic age of legal adulthood.

You have three main jobs until you are legally an adult.

- Keep your room clean
- Go to school (and do well)
- Have respect for others (especially adults)

Think you can handle all that? For some of you, keeping your room clean seems to be completely impossible. It's one room! Stop your sniveling Cadet Sailor; I have to clean an entire house.

Adults have a lot going on so give them a break. They have to go to work, pay the bills, deal with their bosses and worry about you 24/7. They have to make sure that you get at least the basics such as food, clothes and medical attention. They have to make sure you get to school, and if you are lucky to soccer, dance lessons or whatever other extracurricular activities your guardians are willing to pay for.

The Fight is on!

Around the age of 14, suddenly your brain kicks into gear and you start to think that you no longer need any help, guidance or anybody telling you what to do. Cadet Sailor, we all went through this. You and your friends are not the only teenagers who didn't want to listen to anyone and who thought they knew it all. I thought I knew it all, and in reality I didn't know squat. Of course I didn't figure this out until sometime later in life. So let me save you some trouble and time.

Stop fighting the system and learn to survive. We all know that you want independence and it's so close you can see it. To survive four years of "captivity" you will need some tools. First off, let's look at your "captors." They are those pesky adults that are dictating your every move. They watch where you go and tell you what time to be in. They tell you what you can and cannot wear. They won't let you get that tattoo or piercing. They put you through incredible tortures by making you do the dishes or take out the garbage. It's awful and you don't know how you are going to make it through this madness. Suck it up Cadet Sailor, you are in captivity and until you are legally an adult you are under ownership.

That's the way it's been since the dawn of man and if you choose to have kids it will be the same for them. However, having teenagers isn't all it's cut out to be. Just as you are a captive, your captors can't kick you out. They are bound by law to take care of you until you are an adult. In essence, you and your parents are being held captive. Think about that!

Who are your Captors?

They are your parents or guardians of course. These days, extended family members such as aunts, uncles and grandparents have taken on the responsibility of taking care of kids. Some kids are being cared for by foster parents. For the sake of this manual, we are going to call all of them parents.

By nature, parents worry about their kids. They can't help it, it's in the DNA and is the natural order of things. The worry mechanism is so strong, it overrides all thinking. When a parent gets really worried, it can be misconstrued as anger and craziness. They will yell and scream and restrict you from your favorite things but it's often the only way they know of to keep you from harm. Hop into my time machine and I'll take you on a little tour.

1960

Kid: "Mom, can I to go out with my friends tonight?"

Parent: "No, it's a school night and you have homework."

Kid: "Gee wiz Mom, all the kids are going."

Parent: "I said no and that's that."

Kid: "That's not fair."

Parent: "Life's not fair."

Kid: Stomps off to room, slams the door and turns on record player.

Parent: Rolls eyes and starts dinner.

1976 (this was me)

Kid: "Is it alright if I go to San Francisco with some friends to see a concert?"

Parent: "There is no way I'm going to let you drive all the way to San Francisco with those kids."

Kid: "All my friends' parents are letting them go."

Parent: "I'm not all your friends' parents and I said no."

Kid: "That just sucks." Runs to the kitchen, drags the 20 foot phone cord into the laundry room, calls friends to tell them how much her parents suck and plans a "sneak out."

Parent: Rolls eyes and starts dinner.

1996 (me to my son)

Kid: "Why can't I stay out past midnight?"

Parent: "I want you home by midnight because I'm worried for your safety."

Kid: "I can take care of myself; I don't understand why you are so worried all the time."

Parent: "You get your butt home before midnight or you won't be going out at all, oh and by the way, I don't like that kid you hang out with that has the green hair."

Kid: "I hate you; can I get my ear pierced?"

Parent: "No!"

Kid: "I hate you." Runs to room, slams door, and phones friends to plan a "sneak out."

Parent: Rolls her eyes and starts dinner.

Today

You: "I don't understand why I can't run around all night long with my friends."

Your Parent: "I want you home by midnight because I'm worried for your safety."

You: "I can take care of myself; I don't understand why you are so worried all the time."

Your Parent: "You get your butt home before midnight or you won't be going out at all, oh and by the way, I don't like that kid you hang out with that has the green hair."

You: "I hate you, can I get a tattoo?"

Your Parent: "No!"

You: Runs to room, slams door, and turns I-Pod up full blast and text friends to plan a "sneak out."

Your Parent: Rolls her eyes and starts dinner.

Two things – it sucks being a teen and it sucks being a parent. You think you were the only teen who wasn't allowed to run the town at all hours of the night? You're not, so get over it Cadet Sailor!

As with all wars, they eventually come to some sort of end or resolution. Before someone gets hurt, think about some sort of truce, peace treaty or cease fire. Besides, while in captivity you can't do much about your circumstances unless you can persuade a judge to emancipate you. I'll get into that later.

Read the book, "Out of Captivity." It's the story of three American workers who were taken hostage by Colombian rebels. Rebels kept these men among other hostages for over five years, marching them around the Colombian jungles from one makeshift camp to another. They marched for days through dense jungles, had to wear chains around their necks and contracted every jungle disease imaginable. However, somehow they managed to endure their circumstances and learned how to get along with their captors in order to survive until they were rescued. They played the ultimate game of "Survivor." How bad can your captivity be? Unless you are the subject of abuse, and I hope you will reach out and get help if you are, your captivity in no way compares to what these men and women endured in the Colombian jungle. Just think about these people the next time you feel enslaved because you had to take the garbage out or mow the lawn. When you are a legal adult you will be free to do anything you want! Hurray! You can get a job, pay your own bills and join the rest of us in the long hard climb up the mountain of life.

High School Compound

So, you've figured out how to survive your captivity at home, but as part of your captivity you are forced to go to a place called high school. It's the place where all teens congregate to conspire about combat tactics, complain about their parents and teachers (who are co-conspirators in your captivity) and to show off the latest fashions. Sometimes, teens are there to learn.

News flash Cadet Sailor, the law says you have to go to School at least until you are 16 (in most states) when you are eligible for a GED. So guess what, you gotta go! You will not only learn subjects like Math, English, History, etc., but you will also learn and develop social behavior. Social behavior is that thing where you learn to get along and deal with other people. You learn to "play the game of life." Love it or hate it but we gotta do it.

Your main goal in high school should be to get that coveted piece of paper that says you are a high school graduate. Since there are certain requirements for graduation, don't wait until the last minute to see if you are meeting all of them. I've had friends and relatives who sent out graduation announcements only to find out they didn't have enough credits to graduate. How embarrassing! Don't let this situation happen to you. If you are planning to attend a university, make sure you know what prerequisite courses are needed. Major universities will not accept you if you don't take the right classes in high school. If college is something you want to pursue, you need to talk to a high school counselor immediately who will help you choose the classes that are required for college admission. Since you will have to take extra classes to get into a university, be prepared to take summer school.

I will now give you the tactics to survive high school. High school has three major components.

Work – Teachers – Social

Work

Remember your three main jobs mentioned earlier? One of them was doing well in school. Your job is to learn. Learning basic things will help you obtain and hold down a job. You know, J.O.B. It's that thing that pays you money so you can eat and have a roof over you. Unless you come from a rich family you are going to need some form of employment. Well guess what Cadet Sailor, if you can't read or write you'll probably end up with a job that's not as fulfilling as you would like it to be! Dishwasher is a noble job, but you won't want to do that job forever would you? Dishwashers don't get paid much either. I've had my share of crummy low paying jobs but because I have an education, I didn't have to stay at those low paying crummy jobs for long. I can guarantee that without a basic high school education your options for a great job are limited.

There are all sorts of mandatory subjects that you'll probably never ever use in your working life, but you'd be surprised what gets filed away in your brain that you will need to pull out later. Maybe you are playing a trivia game and you have to answer the question: "In what continent is France located?" You will be jumping up and down knowing the answer because you went to school and learned something.

I like to look at the brain as one big giant file room. As you get older all sorts of information gets stored in filing cabinets in your brain.

Files of all kinds are stored, such as facts, things you learned in school, things people have said, things you want to forget, fun times, family vacations, etc. All of that information is stored in your brain's complex filing system. When we are young, there are only a few filing cabinets filled with basic knowledge and not many memories. As we get older, those cabinets get filled up quickly. By the time we are in our 30s there are so many files and filing cabinets in our brains that we have to start doing some housecleaning. Information gets archived in the dark recesses of our big file room and we have to move filing cabinets around to get to certain information. Sometimes we have to do some heavy lifting to get to stored files. Many times, the information gets so buried we are never able to pull it out.

Cadet Sailors, I'm going to rummage around in my file room and pull out some really old files just for you. Hmm…high school years, where is that file? Boy it's crowded in here. College, nope that's not it. Ah here it is. It's the one with all the peace signs and smiley faces. It's pretty dusty too. Let me blow the dust of this file and share what I have learned.

The first thing I'm going to teach you is actually coming from my college file. Not the college file from the days when I went to college right out of high school, that file is a mess! I'm pulling the college file from when I went back to college at age 32. That file is highly organized because I'd gotten my act together by then.

I took a class called "How to Go to School." It was a mandatory class and I thought it was pretty ridiculous that I had to take that class at my age. I had spent 13 years going to school, why would I need such a class? Well Cadet Sailor, I learned so much from that class that I was angry they didn't offer this class in high school. I learned that I was "The Organizer." Once I learned that I was "The Organizer", I excelled in school. I eventually learned to use these learning concepts later in my working career.

Learning new things is a natural process that the brain knows how to do. However, everyone's brain is different.

Just imagine a big door that leads to your big file room in your brain. Much like the door to your house, only one key fits. You now need to find the key that fits in the door to your brain.

The Art of Learning

There are Three Different Types of Learners

The listener –Auditory
The Organizer –Visual
The Doer –Kinesthetic

The Listener

If you remember every single thing that is told to you and are able to pass a test from what you heard, you are The Listener.

You have an uncanny tape recorder running in your head and remember all sorts of facts figures and you visualize concepts as they are being told to you.

You rarely take notes, and when you do they are scribbled down bullet points. The Listener is lucky as they don't use a lot of paper.

The Listener doesn't need a lot of visual explanation of things as they just "get it" by hearing it. The Listener loves to watch films in class and is very focused on listening to the lecture.

The Listener rarely daydreams and does pretty well in class. The Listener has one draw back. Since The Listener is tuned into sound, other sounds such as people talking in class, a book or pen being dropped, a slamming of a door can distract The Listener.

The Listener is most likely having a hard time reading this very book and would rather listen to an audio version. It's a good idea that The Listener takes a tape recorder to class and records the lesson to hear later.

The Organizer

The Organizer (or visual learner) has to see things in Technicolor in order to understand and process information. They have to actually see things in order to learn. The Organizer will have many notebooks and a bag of colored highlighters, pencils, index cards and other props to use to construct notes. The Organizer loves to hang out in the school and office supply section at stores. The Organizer's notes are works of art complete with graphs, pictures, and diagrams and each subject will have its own notebook. The Organizer likes to make studying fun and will use colorful flashcards to memorize facts for a test. I learned that I am The Organizer. As you can see by reading this book, I like to emphasize my point using pictures.

The Organizer probably is enjoying reading this book since it contains fun photos and graphics. The drawback of being The Organizer learner is that so much time is spent drawing, creating and getting notes just right that some of the lecture can get missed. It's a good idea for The Organizer to take a tape recorder to class or even a video camera if the teacher lets you.

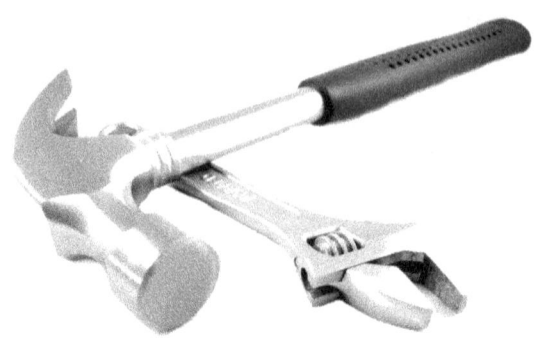

The Doer

The Doer is much like The Organizer as you too like to make pretty notes. However in order for you to learn, you have to actually do the work or problem yourself in order to get it to stick in your head. In subjects like math, you will have "to do" the problems yourself in order to learn. You love classes like biology or art because you are actually doing something in class. You love "to do." The problem with being The Doer: you don't get enough time and attention actually doing the subject during class and you can get behind if you don't understand something. The Doer may need extra help outside of the classroom in order to get more "do" time. You will either have to find a tutor, join a study group or hang out with a friend who can help you with a particular subject. Another option is to ask the teacher, but that's not as much fun as hanging out with a friend.

So, have you figured out what kind of learner you are? If you think you are a little of all three, you might be right. You might be The Doer in math, but in history you may be The Listener. However, most people are more dominate in one learning type overall.

Red Alert! Red Alert! Red Alert! All Hands on Deck, Man Overboard!!!

Are you a victim of abuse? Are you having drama in your life? Are you just sad in general and can't figure out why? All of these things will affect your ability to learn and get through school and life. Sometimes, life can be a bowl of rotten tomatoes and you are swimming around in that mess with no life jacket.

Cadet Sailor, you need to yell help and send out an S.O.S. now. Yell it loud! There is someone out there that will throw you a lifeline, I promise. Don't swim in that lonely ocean alone or YOU WILL DROWN. Tell a friend, tell a teacher, tell your parents, tell SOMEONE. We need you on this ship in order to set sail!

If you are having trouble keeping your concentration, can't remember things no matter how much you try, words get scrambled or are out of focus, tell a teacher, parent or doctor immediately!

It might be something as simple as needing glasses. However, it might be that you have a disorder or some sort of issue that needs attention.

There are a few disorders out there that can be extremely debilitating and affect your ability to learn and comprehend. While many disorders are diagnosed at a very early age, some disorders don't manifest themselves, or don't get noticed until later in life. I've had friends that weren't diagnosed with certain disorders until well into adulthood. They were labeled as lazy students. Teachers and doctors have come a long way in detecting these things early but sometimes things fall through the cracks. There are all sorts of learning disorders out there and I'm going to name just a few.

- **Dyslexia** is a disorder where your brain isn't processing things correctly. Dyslexia has many symptoms but one of the most common is that words and phrases get jumbled up making it almost impossible to read. A friend of mine who has Dyslexia says that when he sees a word he really has to stare at it a long time to get the letters back in order. He said it's like trying to read a jumble puzzle where letters or words are all mixed up and you have to try and figure out what the word really is.

- **Attention Deficit Disorder** (ADD) & **Attention Deficit Hyperactivity Disorder** (ADHD) makes it almost impossible to concentrate and stay focused.

- **Obsessive Compulsive Disorder** (OCD) is another debilitating learning obstacle. You have unwanted thoughts and repetitive, ritualized behaviors you feel compelled to perform. If you have OCD, you probably know that your obsessive thoughts and compulsive behaviors are irrational – but you can't help but perform them. People with OCD have a really hard time getting through day-to-day routines.

If things just don't seem right, TELL SOMEONE! Doctors can help you with medication or therapy. Nip these things NOW before they get out of hand.

Quiz
True or False

A) The Organizer loves colored pencils._____

B) The Listeners love to take notes._____

C) Your brain is one big dining room._____

D) The Doer most likely likes to build stuff._____

E) "Out of Captivity" took place in France._____

Fill in the Blanks

F) What happens around the age of 14? _____

_____

G) When should you yell for help and send out an S.O.S.?

_____

H) What are your three jobs? _____

_____

I) Name one disorder that makes learning difficult._____

J) Why do you need school? _____

Extra Credit: What kind of learner are you?

_____

TEACHERS

Not all are lizards

When I was in school I had teachers that I was convinced were lizards from another planet disguised as human. I swear I saw one of my English teachers catch a fly with her six foot lizard tongue. As I grew older and some of my friends became teachers I realized that they are humans just like you and me. Seriously, I'm not kidding. They are human. It's hard to believe but absolutely true. They don't bleed green or have lizard tongues.

Teachers are co-conspirators with your parents regarding your captivity as a teenager. However, teachers are getting paid to conspire and since you are a captive, it is the teacher's job to make sure you are educated before you are set free. It is your teacher's job to fill up your filing cabinets. Since we have now discovered that teachers are indeed human, I'll try to explain them a little further.

Teachers are PEOPLE that have families, dreams, ambitions, hobbies and problems just like everyone else. They might even have a teenager or two of their own at home. They are faced with budget cuts in the schools, political agendas of their bosses and school boards, expanding class sizes and no pay raises. To top it all off, they have to put up with teenagers eight hours a day five days a week.

Just as there are different types of learners, there are different types of teachers. I'm sure you can come up with a profile of your own teachers, but here are some of the observations I have made as a student and the mother or guardian of a student. I have met many types of teachers and have had to learn to deal with their personalities, strengths and weaknesses both as a student and as a parent. The bottom line is that teachers are being paid to teach you. It is their responsibility to get their job done.

If you are uninterested, bored or are struggling to learn, it is their job to help you get excited or to understand. Yes, there are students who are entirely out of control.

They have behavioral problems that no matter what, the teacher can't fix. However, the teacher chose his/her profession so it is their job to deal with the good, and the bad. If a teacher thought that each and every one of their students was going to be a well behaved perfect angel that teacher was completely misled. That teacher could have very easily gone off and become an accountant or something else. Instead they chose to teach. The teacher can quit and go do something else at any time. YOU, on the other hand, did not choose to go to school. In most states, the law is making you go until you are at least 16 when you are eligible to take the General Equivalency Diploma (GED). You are the captive. So you have to make the best of the situation and figure out a way to get the most out of your teacher. Remember those guys in Colombia?

When teachers do their job of teaching and mentoring and you do your job by getting your assignments done, passing your tests and getting decent grades, everyone will get out alive. You will hopefully get out wearing a cap and gown and holding a diploma.

TEACHER'S JOB

Is the teacher doing what they are paid to do? Let's find out by answering these questions.

Do I love listening to everything this teacher has to say?

Do I get excited about going to their class every day?

Does this teacher make me love school?

Does my teacher explain things clearly?

Does my teacher have patience?

Will I remember this teacher the rest of my life?

Does my teacher make learning boring subjects fun?

Does my teacher really care about my future?

If you answered yes to every question, your teacher is doing a great job.

YOUR JOB

Are you doing your job?

Are you listening?

Are you taking good notes?

Are you asking questions when you don't understand?

Are you completing all of your assignments?

Are you NOT procrastinating?

Are you still reading this?

Are your teeth green?

Do your feet smell?

If you answered yes to the last two questions you have some problems that need attention!

OK, you get the picture. You have to do some work to not only learn, but to figure out your teacher and how to get the most out of them. So, here we go!

Below is a short list of teacher personality types that I have encountered over the years. This list does not cover every single teacher personality that is out there, but I'm sure most of you have encountered at least one of these teachers in the past.

> **Super Teacher**
> **I'm Not a People Person Teacher**
> **Paycheck Teacher**
> **Angry Psycho Teacher**

Super Teacher

The Super Teacher loves being a teacher. They have a passion for teaching and molding the minds of their students. The Super Teacher will go out of their way to reach each and every student and to find out what makes them tick. The Super Teacher wants to know what motivates their students and truly loves each kid as if they were their own. This teacher will put on a costume and act out the American Revolution if that's what it takes for you to learn and remember the lesson.

The Super Teacher will make a subject as mundane as "how to fold a paper bag" seem like the most interesting topic you have ever heard. The Super Teacher always remembers why they wanted to be a teacher in the first place.

I had a history teacher in high school that flew his own plane over the entire stretch of the Oregon Trail, filming the entire journey. Through those films, we were able to see and relive what the pioneers in covered wagons endured all those years ago. I told myself in high school that I was going to see the Oregon Trail for myself one day which I did, all because of that one Super Teacher.

The Super Teacher is a rare breed and there aren't many of them. They don't let the struggles of their life or job politics get in the way of their passion for teaching. You will remember a Super Teacher for the rest of your life.

The I'm Not a People Person Teacher

The I'm not a People Person Teacher (INPP) is academically smart, has a passion for their learned subject matter and loves to teach it to others. But, this teacher never really learned how to properly convey their knowledge to their students in an exciting way. Their teaching style is dry and boring. What this teacher lacks is the personality or "people skills" to deal with the personalities of his or her students. This type of teacher will not go out of their way to motivate their students since they firmly believe the subject they are teaching should be motivation enough.

The INPP teacher thinks that everyone wants to know what they know! Unless you, the student, are already motivated to learn and interested in the subject, you will find this teacher's classes to be boring and you will find yourself watching the clock. The INPP teacher may have the tendency to talk way over your head making the subject seem more complicated. If you are having trouble with learning a subject in the class, the INPP teacher will seem unapproachable or disinterested in you. This is far from the truth. You might be hesitant to get the extra help you need from this teacher. Remember, this teacher has a passion for his or her subject. They will love to talk to you so make it a point to get up there and say "I really love math, but I'm having some trouble and I hope you can help me." The INPP teacher heard three of those words the loudest: "I love Math." You will see a light in their eyes. Say it again. "I love Math, but I need a little help." I swear if you start your sentence with "I love (subject)" you'll start seeing some personality. It shows you have a commonality with this teacher because they love the subject too! This works, trust me.

The Paycheck Teacher

The story of the Paycheck Teacher is a sad one so get out your Kleenex. Once upon a time the Paycheck Teacher dreamed of being a teacher, went to college, worked hard, took all the tests, became a teacher and then something dreadful happened…. life. The Paycheck Teacher now has a mortgage, kids, bills, a boss that gives them grief, a bad marriage, and all sorts of other distractions. The Paycheck Teacher gets up out of bed, puts on a sweat suit, barely rakes a comb through their hair and heads to another day of the dreaded J.O.B. to deal with a classroom of inattentive, hard to manage, unappreciative teenagers. The Paycheck Teacher is grouchy. If you aren't doing your assigned work and are messing around, the Paycheck Teacher won't try to figure out what motivates you. He/she will just call your parents and tell them what a screw-up you are.

The Paycheck Teacher lives for the end of the school day, the weekend, holidays and summer vacation breaks. The bottom line is that the Paycheck Teacher is just there to collect, you guessed it, a paycheck. The Paycheck Teacher needs some love. If you want to get the most out of this Teacher then make friends even if you don't really like him/her. You only have to be "friends" for a few months, so suck it up and make it work. Stay after class and work up a conversation. Tell them what your plans are for the weekend. Tell them that you want to go to college and need some advice. Ask them if they have kids or a dog. Make them see that you are an enjoyable person that is fun to work with. What you are doing is establishing a relationship and hopefully you will be one of the bright spots in his/her day. Prove yourself to the Paycheck Teacher and they will go the extra mile to help you however they can. You are now co-workers instead of student and teacher. Both of you are doing your jobs, you are learning and the teacher is teaching.

Angry Psycho Teacher

Boy, have I had my share of Angry Psycho Teachers. Teachers that throw things, yell, scream and back in the old days when it was "legal," slam a student up against a wall. An Angry Psycho Teacher can make your life a virtual hell. These teachers have serious issues and probably shouldn't be around kids or anyone else for that matter. These teachers are plain angry and you are an easy target. If you are stuck with one of these teachers who has at least one meltdown a week, use some of the tactics described above for the Paycheck Teacher. Make friends with the monster and it might not eat you. If that doesn't work, get all of your work done, shut your mouth in class, don't make eye contact and stay off their radar. It's about survival!

Whatever you do, don't get into a screaming match with this teacher as it will only make things worse and you will find yourself sitting in the principle's office, or suspended. If this teacher gets physical with you, by all means report it to law enforcement. Physically handling or striking another person is against the law.

As you can see, there are a few different personality types when it comes to teachers. Whatever type you are dealing with, remember you are in the game of "Survivor." Make the best of the situation and try and figure out the best tactic to get your teacher's attention and to gain their favor. There is absolutely nothing wrong with being teacher's pet if that's what it takes to get a good grade and the extra help you need. The goal in the end is to graduate and gain your freedom. If you learn how to get the most out of your teachers, you can use these tools later down the road when you are dealing with other people, such as your bosses or co-workers.

Quiz
True or False

A) A Super Teacher is excited about teaching._____

B) A Paycheck Teacher is distracted by life._____

C) An INPP Teacher loves their subject of expertise._____

D) Arguing with an Angry Psycho Teacher might get you suspended._____

Fill in the Blanks

E) I can get a INPP Teacher to help me by _____
_____

F) Super Teachers do extra things in class such as_____
_____

G) The Paycheck Teacher will most likely take an interest in me if I_____

Extra Credit: The name of my Super Teacher is_____. He/she is a Super Teacher because
_____
_____
_____
_____
_____.

SOCIAL

As you start to mature a thing starts to grow inside. No not that! Get your mind out of the gutter. Along with your height and other body parts, (you're in the gutter again), there is something that gets really big and it's called The Ego. Sigmund Freud, a super smart psychiatrist who lived a long time ago has a really long description of the Ego which you can research for yourself if you are really interested in all that mumbo jumbo.

In a nutshell, your Ego is what drives your personality, your wants and your emotions. Have you heard someone say, "He has such a huge Ego?" They are saying that the person has an overly high opinion of themselves which can be a little offensive to others. This gives your Ego a bad rap. Your Ego can become a big hairy monster if you let it. Having a high opinion of yourself is a good thing! Seriously, it is! Just don't go out of your way to make yourself appear better than others because that's what makes people annoyed with you. Embrace and love your Ego – feed your Ego! Your Ego loves to belong. Your Ego loves to be loved. Your Ego is YOU!

The Ego Needs a Home!

Nerds, Geeks, Jocks, Preppies, Emos, Skaters, Goths, Stoners, Rednecks and YOU

Just like a puppy, your Ego needs to be nurtured and fed. And just like a puppy, your Ego needs to be trained! Have you ever seen someone with a puppy on a leash and the puppy is taking that person for a walk? The puppy is dragging their human down the street totally out of control. Don't let your Ego take you for a walk! Get your Ego trained and you will both walk calmly together through life's big doggie park! Your Ego will immediately want to hang out with cool Egos. Take your Ego by the leash and give it a good yank. Your Ego isn't trained; it has no idea what's cool and what isn't.

Keep asking your Ego these questions:

- Is hanging out with this group of Egos going to benefit me in the long run? (Help me to my end goal, freedom)
- Will I be associated with these Egos long after high school?
- Are the actions of these Egos legal? Will they get me in trouble?
- Where will these other Egos be in 10 years and do I want to be with them or like them in 10 years?

Having been a high school survivor myself a zillion years ago I can tell you things were pretty much the same back then. We had the stoners, jocks, popular kid cliques, nerds, and all the rest. Schools today have the same groups and a few new ones have been added over the years. Your Ego loves cool! It wants to belong and your Ego can get you into a lot of trouble if you don't train it wisely! If you know a little about dogs, you know they roam in packs and and the pack has a leader. I live in the country and have seen domesticated dogs get into a pack. In the pack, they start committing crimes, digging into garbage and killing other animals such as livestock. The animal control officer will then come out, round up the pack and haul them to the pound. Some of these dogs will go back to their rightful owners, get some training and die old and happy. Some of these dogs will be put to sleep. Don't let this happen to you. Letting your puppy Ego get caught up in this pack mentality will lead you right to jail or possibly death. Don't be stupid – get control of your Ego. You are the boss and since you are a Captain in training, eventually you will have to train that Ego to drive your ship. So, surround yourself with other smart Captains and not loser snarling, rabid pack dogs! Got it Matey? Woof! (that's dog for keep reading.)

Just say No. First Lady Nancy Reagan used this slogan in her anti-drug campaign a long time ago. Guess what? A lot of my friends never said no! Yep, they ignored our First Lady. They didn't know the First Lady so what did they care what she had to say. So a lot of my friends said yes! I got a lot of pressure from my friends to say yes right along side of them. So, I said yes a few times. That was pretty stupid! I followed along like a stupid zombie sheep. Sheep have to follow other sheep, it's just in their DNA. My mother used to say "If they told you to jump off a cliff would you do it?" Well NO, I'm not that stupid. However, saying yes to things I knew were wrong was just like following them over a cliff.

I speak from experience Cadet Sailors. My Ego wanted to belong with the other Egos so bad that it was willing to sacrifice everything, including my safety. As I learned later in life, real friends wouldn't give a rat's behind if I said, "No, I'll Pass." I was extremely lucky that I never got addicted to anything like some of my friends did. I was pretty young at the time and luckily snapped out of my zombie trance. I won't lie to you, drugs and alcohol give you the "Superman" feeling, however even Superman had kryptonite that could destroy him! Substance abuse has destroyed many families and lives. Some of my friends and relatives have alcohol and drug problems that began in high school. High school students don't expect to become addicted when they try drugs or alcohol, but the substance doesn't know that!

Listen to Nancy! JUST SAY NO!

Stop being a weak zombie sheep!

Get Involved

If you are going to run with a pack of Egos, it's best to run with a pack that is doing something constructive. Join a club or organization that interests you. I was shy in high school and I had a hard time approaching people that I didn't know. I found that joining clubs and sports helped me get over my shyness since I was constantly meeting and working with new people. I joined a back packing club that took hiking trips all over the high Sierra mountains in California. I learned all sorts of important and lifesaving lessons about camping and hiking in the wilderness that I still remember and use today. I was also involved in sports and other organizations outside of school. If you are planning on going to college, having an affiliation with community oriented organizations and clubs will make your college applications impressive. Organizational memberships are also impressive on job applications. Prospective employers are impressed with people who show initiative by getting involved in clubs and organizations. This shows you are a team player and outgoing. Running for a position in student government is another way to gain some valuable experience and friends. Holding a school political office also looks good on a job or college application. It shows you are a leader.

Home School and Independent Study

Is That What Floats Your Boat?

Some students excel in traditional school where they have the social interaction with teachers and other students to learn new things. Other students thrive on doing things in a more isolated environment. Home school and independent study programs have been found to be extremely helpful in getting high school students to the ultimate goal of graduation.

Some students have too much energy and get distracted easily when they have to sit in a classroom seven to eight hours a day. Some students get so caught up in the social aspects of high school, peer pressure or are the targets of bullying that staying home is the only option. In traditional school, you have to go to class every day, listen to lectures and instructions for up to seven hours and then do most of the actual assignments at home, after school hours. Add that up and you are actually going to school five days a week - 10 hours a day. You are spending a lot of time at school, but you can only work as fast as the semester will let you.

In home school or independent study programs, students will meet with an instructor once or twice a week to get instructions and assignments. Students are then able to work on their assignments at home and can usually get them finished in just a few hours. Another nice thing about home school or independent study is the flexibility of the assignments and course work.

My son was having a terrible time in traditional school. He was always getting into trouble, talking and messing around in class. He had too much energy to sit through eight hours of school. Frustrated with his horrible grades, we made the decision to pull him out of traditional high school and get him enrolled in a charter home school program. The situation was ideal since I worked early mornings and afternoons and was home during the day to monitor the situation. Home school may not work for you unless you are completely self motivated and can get your work done without someone watching over you all day. My son became a straight "A" student for the first time in his life. He loved doing his lessons and really enjoyed writing papers on documentaries he watched on cable TV. The home school curriculum also gave him time during the day to work an internship at a graphics art studio. Don't think that home school is easier, it isn't. You are driving your own boat in home school and if you aren't careful, you can easily run out of gas if you don't manage your time well.

Do you feel as if you don't have enough time to get everything you want accomplished? IMPORTANT! If you don't learn how to manage your time now, it will only get worse for you when you are an adult and have a hundred more things on your plate. Teachers will pile on the homework and you have a part-time job and chores to do at home. You would also like to have some time to mess around on the Internet or watch TV. You can do all of this if you are smart! If you procrastinate, things will get out of hand and you will feel like you are on a runaway train with no breaks. Before you know it, your assignments are due, you haven't started on any of them and you are in serious danger of getting an "F." It's not impossible to get a handle on any of this if you decide you want to take control of the runaway train. Time management is pretty easy if you sit down and write yourself a schedule.

Purchase some sort of calendar or Day Planner at any stationary store. If you can't afford one of these, make your own calendar out of binder paper and keep it in a notebook.

1. Write down the days when your assignments are due.

2. Plan each day with a schedule of the things you need to do and would like to do. Remember the "Need To" things must get priority.

3. Try and plan some play time so you don't feel overwhelmed or deprived.

4. Stick to your schedule.

Don't have the "I'll do it tomorrow" attitude. Have the "I'll get it done right now" attitude and you will achieve all of your goals.

Quiz
True or False

A) Your Ego is like an untrained puppy._____
B) Your Ego will want to hang out with other Egos and do stupid things._____
C) Your Ego will take you for a walk if you let it._____
D) Your Ego is you._____
E) Nancy Reagan was the Queen of England._____
F) When dogs roam in packs they have a tendency to get in trouble._____

Fill In the Blanks

G) Just like a puppy, your Ego needs to be_____
_____

H) Your Ego is what drives your_____
_____

I) In order to do well in a home school program, you must have _____

J) Home school students have flexibility with their_____
_____

Extra Credit: Describe how you currently manage your time.
_____
_____
_____
_____
_____
_____

Part 2

Start Building Your Boat

Your boat is made out of your experiences and skills. The more skills you have, the sturdier the boat. You'll learn to drive, possibly take on the responsibility of work and hopefully will start earning the trust of others. In order to sail off to freedom and the rest of your life as an adult you must first build a good boat. Without a sturdy boat you will sink. Those waters are shark infested and very cold.

Licensed To Drive

The coveted driver license is a privilege, not a right. YES PRIVILEGE!! The DMV giveth and the police can taketh away. Americans have had a love affair with cars since they were invented in the late 1800s. Teenagers have been dreaming of getting a driver license since the invention of these wheeled marvels. A driver license is your ticket to ultimate freedom and independence. You drive, therefore you are cool.

RED ALERT, RED ALERT, ALL HANDS ON DECK!

Don't be a Crash Test DUMMY!

FACT: Car crashes are the number one cause of death of young people between the ages 16 and 20.

FACT: 16-year-old drivers have a higher crash rate than drivers of any other age.

FACT: 16-year-old drivers are three times more likely to die in a car crash than the average of all drivers.

FACT: Statistics show that 16-and 17-year-old driver death rates increase with each additional passenger.

(Statistics from the National Highway Traffic Safety Administration, www.nhtsa.dot.gov)

CARS = MISSILES WITH WHEELS

The average passenger car weighs between 3000 and 4,500 pounds – that's a big hunk of projectile!

Missile: an object (as a weapon) thrown or projected usually so as to strike something at a distance. (Merriam-Webster Dictionary)

Motor Vehicle: an automotive vehicle not operated on rails; especially one with rubber tires for use on highways. (Merriam-Webster Dictionary)

When you look at the definition from the dictionary of these two things, they seem quite different. However, a missile and a car have some similarities.

Missile – made of metal

Motor Vehicle – made of metal

   Missile – propelled to go at great speeds

   Motor Vehicle – propelled to go at great speeds

Missile – causes destruction when it hits an object

Motor Vehicle– causes destruction when it hits an object

   Missile – can be used as a weapon

   Motor Vehicle – can be used as a weapon

Did you Know?

If you are going 60 miles per hour in your car, and you have to slam on your breaks for any reason, you won't come to a complete stop until you are 282 feet down the road! A football field is 360 feet, so it will almost take you most of a football field to stop if nothing is in your way. So, if you are going 90 miles per hour it will take you more than a football field to stop. If something is in your way while you are going 90 miles per hour you are now a weapon of mass destruction and the results will be devastating. If you are driving on wet and slick roads, it will take you three times the distances to stop your missile. This means that you should drive slower when weather is bad and roads are slick.

The very sad but true story of Lesley Suthard.

Three lives were cut short because a speeding teenager was messing around on the road while going to get ice cream with his friends.

Twenty-year-old Lesley, a bright young woman full of life, was on her way home one night. She was minding her own business, traveling on her side of the freeway completely unsuspecting of the dangerous person that was driving on the opposite side of the freeway.

A car came across the center divide and hit Lesley head-on instantly killing her and the two occupants in the other car. The driver that hit Lesley was a teenager that was goofing around in his car and speeding over 90 miles per hour. The two teens in the speeding missile were on their way to get ice cream and thought it would be fun to race another carload of friends on the freeway. However, the small compact car they were driving wasn't made for racing, nor was the driver experienced in driving a race-car. Their car went out of control and sped across the freeway to the other side where Lesley happened to be at that second.

Lives were lost and families were devastated.

All became national statistics that night and it was all so preventable. Take a good hard look at this photo. This is what happens when two missiles collide.

Lesley's car

In most states, you are eligible to get your learners permit for your driver license at 15 ½ years old. Many states are putting all sorts of restrictions on drivers who are under 18. You can't run around town with your friends and you can't drive at all hours of the night. Studies have shown that taking out all of the "fun" that we all once had in cars is keeping you alive. I kind of like being alive, don't you?

You will spend your entire life behind the wheel of some sort of transportation, and it will be a miracle if you are never in some sort of crash or fender bender. You will be sharing the road with millions upon millions of other drivers. You will share the road with people who speed, talk on their phones, are drunk or on drugs, putting on their makeup and doing their hair, scolding their kids in the backseat and who knows what else. All of these people are sitting in speeding metal missiles that are hurtling down the road. One might be aiming for you when you least expect it. Drive your missile defensively, pay attention and obey the laws. It's not just your life that is in jeopardy, your missile on wheels can kill others.

Unless you live and work in a big city where there is good public transportation, you will be driving a car to get yourself to work or school, so do us all a favor and become a good responsible driver.

Quiz
True or False

A) A car is like a missile. _____
B) 16-year-olds get in more car crashes than any other age group._____
C) Having a driver license is a privilege._____
D) The average car weighs between 3,000 and 4,000 pounds. _____
E) A car can be used as a weapon._____
F) Many states are putting restrictions on teen drivers._____

Fill in the Blanks

G) When traveling 60 miles per hour it takes almost the length of a _____ to stop.
H) Lesley Suthard was killed by a _____.
I) 16-and 17-year-old death rates increase with additional _____ in the car.
J) Lesley Suthard's death could have been prevented if____
_____
K) You are sharing the road with people that are most likely-
_____
_____
_____

Extra Credit: How would you feel if a friend or relative was seriously injured or killed by a careless driver? _____
_____
_____

Show Me the Money!

If you are going to high school full time, it's a little hard to hold down a full-time job and nobody is really asking you to work unless you need to help your family. However, a little bit of work never hurt anyone and working a part-time job will prepare you for life when you are dependent upon your own earnings. Most employers won't hire anyone under 16 and some employers won't hire anyone under 18. Don't let this discourage you since there are still many opportunities to make a little cash on the side. These are all jobs either I or my son did as teenagers. None of these jobs have an age requirement since you are your own boss.

*Babysit on weekends

*Mow lawns

*Rake leaves

*Housework

*Odd jobs for elderly people

*Tutor younger kids

*Pet/house sit

*Wash cars

*If you play an instrument, give lessons

*Design logos or other computer graphics

*Put together websites

*Volunteer work (no pay, but you get experience and it's fulfilling)

*Make and sell crafts (I made painted rock animals and sold them in a consignment shop when I was 14 years old)

This is just a short list of ideas so let your imagination run wild. I sometimes feel sorry for homeless people who come to me begging for money, but I think back at the lawn mowing service that my son started when he was only 12 years old. He made up some flyers and placed them around the neighborhood. The phone started ringing and he took our lawnmower all over the neighborhood mowing lawns. If you really want to make a buck, then get going. If a 12-year-old can make money so can you.

Working will also help you develop the skills necessary to deal with other people, especially bosses. As you are expanding your skills for your journey later in life, you are also learning about something called "work ethic."

Work ethic is the way you handle yourself in the workplace. Don't get a bad reputation of being a total flake. Bosses hate flakes and word will spread like a wildfire that you are a flake if you don't have a good work ethic. Flake = unemployable. Don't let this happen to you.

Good Work Ethic:

Show up to work on time every day.

Give the boss or client plenty of notice if you are going to be late or are not able to make it.

Willingly follow directions of your boss or client without complaint.

When there isn't anything to do, find something to do. This lets your boss know that you are there to work and not stand around.

If you show good work ethic and do your best on the job each and every day, your bosses and clients will happily write letters of recommendation for you to take to your next job.

Get Healthy

You are young and don't have any health problems, so why should you worry about being healthy? Believe it or not, what you do or don't do with your body now will forever haunt you later in life! If you smoke, eat junk, don't exercise, you will most likely continue those bad habits in your adult life. This can lead to serious health problems. If certain diseases run in your family, you need to work harder to stay healthy. Start now Cadet Sailor. We want you around for a long time!

Are you too Fat?

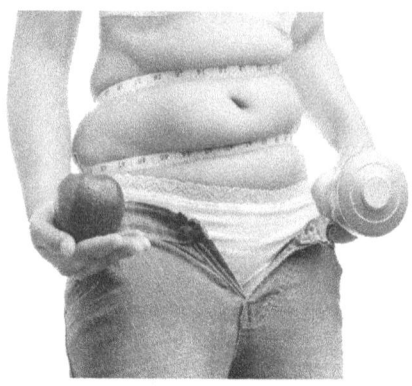

A lot of teens are fat. I use the "F" word to hopefully get your attention. The word overweight doesn't have the shock value that the word FAT has. Are you Fat? Having a little meat on your bones isn't a bad thing but if you have excess "meat"(fat) you could be destined for a lifetime of yo-yo dieting and health issues. It's easier to get a handle on your weight when you are young. Create good eating and exercise habits now.

Obesity: A condition characterized by the excessive accumulation and storage of **fat** in the body. (Merriam-Webster Dictionary)

It is astounding that in the 21st Century people under the age of 30 are fighting obesity. Obese teenagers under the age of 19 represent 15% of the American population. (*Center for Disease Control, www.cdc.gov*)

1. Do you have underlying conditions that are keeping you over-or-under weight? Talk to your doctor. Your body might not be processing your fuel properly.

2. Your doctor can determine what your weight should be according to your height, frame and medical history.

3. How much exercise are you doing? Are you burning all the fuel you are consuming or are you getting enough fuel for your active lifestyle?

Below are just a few of the reasons you don't want to be obese. Obesity leads to:

Reduction in your life span. Yes, you will die earlier than most people.

Heart Disease. Heart disease is the leading cause death in the United States. (*Center for Disease Control*)

Diabetes

It's simple math. Zero movement + too many calories = fat. For some reason in the past several years, people stopped moving. Kids stopped playing outside and quit riding their bikes. Instead, they are sitting in front of the TV or their computers with an open bag of cookies or chips. There are now TV ads telling kids to go outside and play. What has this world come to when kids have to be told to go outside and play? We are a society doomed to health problems and early death.

When people stopped moving, the fast-food industry grew to epic proportions. If you look at any busy intersection you will see a fast food restaurant on every corner. Then came the super-size portions, which consists of giant sized French fries and large sodas. People started consuming more and more calories but didn't start moving enough to burn off those calories.

Just what is a calorie? A calorie is a measure of energy expenditure. Think of your body as a machine that needs fuel. You eat food which contains calories, which is the fuel you need to run your body's machine. Your body can only burn so much fuel a day, and the rest is stored in a reserve tank (usually your stomach, butt and thighs.) To keep your reserve tanks empty, don't take in so much fuel. Take in only the fuel you need to operate. Take in only enough calories that you can burn each day.

So how much fuel do you need to operate? If you are sitting on your butt all day, you don't need much fuel since your body machine isn't working very hard. So quit filling up your tank with excess fuel. If you are an athlete or are, running, climbing and working hard, you will need more fuel than the person who sits. Talk to your doctor or nutrition expert to find out how much fuel or calories you should be consuming in order to maintain your desired body weight. There are all sorts of circumstances that come into play that determine how much fuel you need. There are all sorts of websites where you can calculate how many calories you can have per day to maintain or lose weight. Once you figure out how many calories you are allowed based on your age, how much exercise you do, your height, etc, start tracking the calories you are consuming. Look at the packages of the food you eat. You will be surprised.

You Must Eat!

If you determine that you should lose a few pounds and you've talked to your doctor about it, the worst thing you can do is stop eating to lose weight. Your body will fight you over this. Your body will go into starvation mode and will store every single ounce of fat you have in order to survive.

You might lose a few pounds in the process, but once you start eating your starved body will take every bit of that fuel and store it in the reserve tanks in case it needs it. Your body is a very smart machine and it knows what it needs and doesn't need. It's your brain that needs a little tune up. If you extensively starve your body, it will start eating your muscle and work away at your skeletal system in order to stay alive. You can die from starvation. You need to eat. Talk to your doctor or a nutrition expert about your diet and how much weight you want to lose and they will put you on a balanced healthy program of diet and exercise! You will be surprised at the amount of food you will still be able to eat while still losing weight. Also remember that breakfast is the most important meal of the day. You are burning calories just by doing your normal everyday activities.

Are you too Skinny?

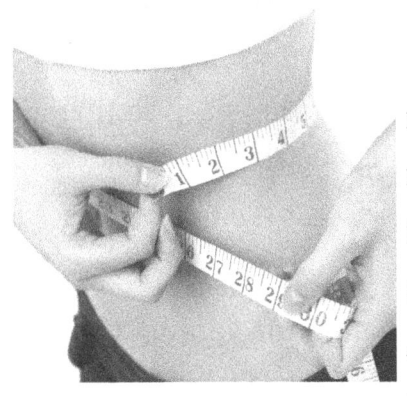

Some people are thin no matter what they eat or how much or little they move. My father is one of those people. (He almost didn't get into the Army because he was under weight.) Their body burns calories fast no matter how much they eat. If you are super skinny and are eating a normal and healthy diet you should be okay. Continue to eat all the right things, proteins, vegetables, the right amount of carbohydrates and you should be fine. However, just because you are naturally skinny doesn't mean you are in the best of physical shape. You still need to exercise to keep your heart and bones healthy. Build some muscle strength by doing a few pushups every day and do some fast walking or jogging a few times a week. If you are concerned about being too skinny, if you are dropping weight drastically or suddenly your energy level is low, consult your doctor immediately.

Get Some Sleep

Saturday mornings are great, you can sleep until noon to catch up on all of the sleep you aren't getting during the week. Staying up all night is great if you are a vampire, however you are a mere mortal and must get up and go to school. The brain needs a good nights sleep so that all of those files can get organized for the next day.

Don't Stress

Being overly stressed out about stuff can affect your health. Your body will start reacting in all sorts of bizarre ways if you are stressed out. If you have tons of drama in your life, feel overwhelmed about school and/or work, talk to someone about it to help you get through whatever it is that's stressing you out. Severe stress can cause severe health issues!

RED ALERT RED ALERT, ALL HANDS ON DECK

Don't believe what you see on the cover of magazines. No one is telling you that you need to be stick thin. Those models on magazine covers have been computer enhanced to make them appear to be super stick skinny which is not healthy either. You need to be healthy. Talk to your doctor as to what your body weight should be. Some people have become so absorbed in being skinny, like those models, that they stop eating or develop crazy eating habits and disorders in order to look like these people in magazines who aren't real.

The Doctor is in

Just like a car, you need to take your body into the shop once in a while to make sure everything is working properly. Just because you are young doesn't mean that your machine can't break down. If you can get in to see a doctor, don't be shy. Tell him or her everything that's bothering you. If you're sad, tell the doctor. If you aren't feeling good, tell the doctor.

If you are having sex, by all means tell the doctor. I know it's embarrassing, but they've heard it all before, so tell them. The doctor can hook you up with all sorts of information, medications and help you take preventative precautions. The doctor can run tests on your engine to see if there are any repairs needed. You should visit with a doctor once a year.

Stay in top shape:

DO: Exercise regularly.
Eat a balanced diet of protein, vegetables, fruits and carbohydrates. (If you don't know what these are, consult the web for all sorts of nutrition information.)
Visit your doctor.
Get to know your body in order to recognize warning signs.

DON'T: Smoke anything! (There is no such thing as a safe cigarette.)
Drink alcohol, (you aren't 21 yet anyway!)
Sit around all day.
Ignore signs that something is wrong.

Stay Fit for Free

or next to free

Get exercise or Yoga DVDs (Buy them used on the Internet or check them out at the library)

Run and walk (roads and stairs are free)

Do sit-ups, push-ups and leg lifts (floor is free)

Jog on a mini-trampoline (mine cost $25.00 new)

Buy some weights at a yard sale (sometimes they are free for the taking)

Use heavy things around the house as weights (free)

Ride your bike (buy a used cheap bike at a yard sale)

Get involved in whatever sports are offered in your school or community, even if you think you suck at it.

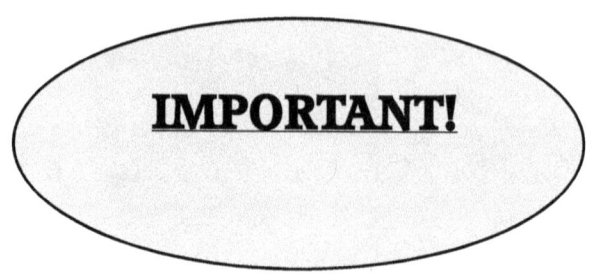

If you haven't exercised in a long time you should talk with your doctor to find out if you have any underlying health conditions. You may have a heart condition and not know it and if you start running or performing other really strenuous exercises, it could be fatal. Check with your doctor if you are really out of shape. Also, you want to start out slow. If you are really out of shape you should start out by going on fast walks then work your way up to running. Remember to always stretch before you work out. If you don't stretch, you may pull a muscle or tendon which is extremely painful and takes a long time to heal.

Quiz
True or False

A) Obesity can cause major health risks._____

B) Exercise will make your bones healthy._____

C) There is an obesity problem in America._____

D) Teens don't need to watch their diet._____

E) The fast food industry is big business._____

F) Your body needs calories to run._____

G) If you are sitting around all day, your body doesn't need a lot of extra fuel._____

Fill in the Blanks

H) If you are losing weight really fast you should_____
_____

I) You should _____
if you are trying to lose weight and having trouble.

J) Models on magazine covers are most likely _____
_____

K) You should visit with your doctor once a _____

Extra Credit: What should you do to stay in good health?
_____
_____
_____

Part 3

Preparing for the Boot

Hear that sound? It's the sound of freedom. Or, it could be the sound of a great big boot coming to kick your butt right out of the house once and for all. You are about to embark on a huge life ahead of you. Some of you will go out and excel right away. You'll go to college, get a degree and go on to a fabulous career. Most of you however, will struggle for a while, some for years, while trying to figure it all out. Whatever you decide, we all have one thing in common. We all get the boot. So let's get prepared!

Learn How to Live Now

Ok Cadet Sailors, if you made it this far in your manual, you are well ahead of the game than most people your age. You've learned how to basically stay alive while you are in your captive environment. However, I bet your parents are doing a lot of the heavy lifting for you. While some teens are learning how to do their own laundry and how to cook a meal, there are many of you that are not. I just watched a news story the other night where college students who have just been booted out of their nests were having to call their parents for mundane things they weren't prepared for. Of course parents are willing to help if they can, however at some point you need to try and figure things out for yourself if you want true independence.

You Gotta Eat

When I was a teen, you couldn't get me near the kitchen when my mother was cooking dinner. I had no interest in cooking whatsoever. However, I was made to do the dishes every single night. I became an expert dishwasher from the time I was able to reach the sink, but I never learned how to cook a meal for myself. When I finally moved out of the house and had my own apartment, I barely knew how to fry an egg.

Do yourself a favor and learn how to make a meal or two. You don't need to become the next super chef, but it helps if you learn how to do some basic cooking so that you can eat healthy meals and stay out of the fast food restaurants. Take a trip to the grocery store and buy some groceries. See if you can buy a weeks worth of meals for $50. Take a calculator to the grocery store and buy meat, bread, vegetables and other goodies that you can make for your breakfast, lunch and dinner for a week. You will be on a tight budget when you move out but you will still have to eat. Learn now how to stretch your grocery dollars.

Get to Know Your Wheels

If you own a car and depend on it to take you back and forth to school and work you better make sure it's in good working order at all times. Do you know how to check the oil in your car? If not, you better learn. If you are low on oil, you could burn up your engine. Learn what those blazing red and yellow lights on your dash mean. Those lights are warning you that your car is very sick and needs to go in for repairs. Find someone who knows about cars that can give you a little tour under the hood. Car engines can look pretty complex when you first open the hood, but when you learn what all of that stuff does it won't seem so scary and foreign to you. When I was in my twenties, I owned a few clunkers and I quickly learned how to do some of the needed repairs myself. I learned how to change the oil and oil filter myself, which saved me lots of money. I learned how to change a tire and I also learned how to change an alternator, fuel pump, belts and a host of other things. When you are a broke young person just starting out, you will be forced to take some matters into your own hands. Learn the basic mechanics now, it will save you time and money later.

Manage your Money

When you get the boot, you are going to have to pay rent, utilities, insurance, car payment, buy groceries, clothes, and a ton of other stuff so that you can live. If you have a job, your money should be going into some sort of checking or savings account. Having a bunch of cash lying around is dangerous since it can be easily stolen or lost. Also, if you are paying everything with cash, you have no idea where your money is going. One day you'll have $40 in your wallet and the next day it will be gone. You won't have a clue where it went. While you are still in high school, open up a checking account with whatever earnings, birthday money or any other cash you have on hand. Typically, you will also get some sort of ATM card so that you can get cash out of your account at a machine.

Be very careful when doing this as you can easily lose track of how much money is in your checking or savings account. The balance on the receipt you get out of the machine is most likely not the real balance of your account. You probably have a lot less in the account than the receipt shows. This is because the check you wrote or the debit transaction you made at the store hasn't cleared the bank yet. If you withdraw more money than you have in your account, your bank will charge you all sorts of fees and fines. Learn how to budget your money and responsibly use your bank account now.

When I first got the boot, I didn't pay too much attention to the checks I was writing and I quickly became overdrawn in my bank account. It was a horrible situation since I ended up owing the bank about $100 in service fees. I had to close my account, borrow some money from a friend to pay off the bank and start over with a new account and new bank. It wasn't a pleasant experience and I blame myself for not learning how to manage a bank account before I moved out.

Getting the boot won't hurt so bad if you do a little planning while you are still in the comfort of your little nest. If you can plan for at least your first two years out of the nest, you are ahead of the game.

Emancipation

As a paralegal I was asked about emancipation many times by both parents and teens. In most states, you are not legally an adult until you are 18 years old. Being a legal adult means that you are completely your own person. You can legally sign a contract, register to vote and legally live on your own. Being emancipated means that you can have some of these things when you are as young as 14. You will still not be able to vote, however if you are emancipated you can legally live on your own and you can sign a contract. Your parents are no longer legally obligated to take care of you. Sounds like a heck of a deal doesn't it? It's not so easy. A judge in a court of law is the only person who can grant you emancipation. You have to prove to the judge that you are totally:

- Living on your own (staying with friends or relatives doesn't count)
- Paying your own bills
- Maintaining lawful employment

If you can prove all of this to a judge you just might get your emancipation. Its all up to a judge and you showing that judge you can totally take care of yourself. It's not easy for a 14-year-old kid to get gainful employment, since at 14 you are still bound by child labor laws. Getting an apartment or place to live on part-time minimum wage is next to impossible. However, I have known people who were emancipated at 16 and were able to show the court they were completely self sufficient. If you've had enough and seriously want to make it out on your own check out www.publiccounsel.org for a detailed list of emancipation requirements.

What to do, What to do

When you are nearing your high school graduation or getting your GED, someone is going to ask you "Well, what are you going to do when you get out?" You think about it for a minute and say, "Go to college, I guess." In actuality, you don't have a clue. You have no plan other than turning 18 and taking off. Where are you going to get money for rent? Where are you going to work? Where are you going to get the money for school? Where are you going to school? It's all so confusing and daunting. Some of you have decided on college while some of you have gone one step further and actually decided on a major of study. However, a lot of you haven't a clue. You just want to get out of high school but have not seen your future beyond that. If you have really nice parents that will let you live at home rent free with no job for the rest of your life, you have it made and have nothing to worry about. That sounds like paradise! I had no desire to live one more minute with my parents after I graduated from high school. I wanted my independence so bad, I could taste it. Let freedom ring!

College, is it for you?

College could be for you, but maybe not right away. If you were studious in high school, got good grades and really enjoyed being in school, you are most likely a good candidate to go immediately into college. If you are a good student in high school, you will probably have a good chance of being accepted in a four year college. Being accepted to a college is getting difficult and you may not be accepted unless you have an excellent grade point average and great SAT scores.

I was a mediocre high school student with average grades and below average SAT scores. I was not accepted to a four year university; however, I was able to attend community college since there are no grade requirements.

If you were like me, a mediocre student, you might want to wait a while to start college. I went to college right out of high school and dropped out after one year. Too much freedom can be your demise if you aren't already a studious type of person and have some self discipline. I let the lure of dorm parties get in the way of my school. I didn't have good study habits already instilled in my brain so I was easily distracted by all the fun and new found freedom. When I went back to school at 32 years old, paying the tuition myself, I had a 4.0 grade point average and absolutely loved school. It was after having lived my life of plugging along that I found school a valuable tool in my quest to make more money. Let me save you some time right now. If you struggled to get through high school, college may not be the best option for you immediately after you graduate. Your parents may not like me saying this to you, however I'm trying to save them some of their hard earned money if they plan on paying your tuition. Frustrated parents tell me all the time that their kid is goofing off in college. That is because their kid is going to college because the parent wanted them to go. You should go to college if you have the desire to go to college. That's the only way it's going to work for you. College will mean more to you if it's YOUR passion. You might not be interested in college because you have no idea what to study once you get there. You figure that if you are going to spend all of that money, you better be sure what you are going to take once you're there.

Don't fret about it. If you want to try your hand at college, you don't have to pick a major right away. Spend the first couple of years completing all of those pesky general education requirements. If you still aren't excited about going to college, take a year off, go to work and you just might figure out that you will eventually need some sort of higher education. After a year of working, you might figure out what interests you. You might get a job as a secretary in a law office and decide you would like to be a paralegal or lawyer. Maybe you get a job working at a restaurant and you decide you want to get into the restaurant management business. Of course these jobs take a college degree, but you will have some sort of motivation to go since you already got a taste of these types of jobs.

Once you decide you are going to go to college, either right out of high school or after you wait a couple of years, you will need to figure out financing. College is very expensive and if your parents aren't going to pay for it, you will need to get educated about college before you step foot onto a college campus.

Paying for College

Government Grants: These are funds that are available from the government. You usually don't have to pay them back. However, these grants are available only to students who are low income. If you are right out of high school, the grant agency will look at your parent's income along with yours. If you and your parents made too much money your grant might be denied. However, some grants might have higher income limits than others so apply for them all.

Other Grants: Some organizations offer grants based on religion, ethnicity or other circumstances.

Student Loans: There are various student loans available at reasonable interest rates. The good part about a student loan is that you don't have to start paying it back until you are done with school. You can also possibly delay paying back the loan while you are unemployed looking for work after you graduate.

Scholarships: These are funds that are available from all sorts of organizations and individuals. Scholarships can be as low as $100 but can be as much as thousands of dollars. Some scholarships will pay your entire way through college. Eligibility for these scholarships varies greatly and most times you will have to apply and compete with others for the same scholarship.

Self Pay: Paying for your own college education will be difficult but not impossible. I've known many people, me included, who paid their own way through college. You may have to work during the day and go to school at night, but you can still accomplish your goals.

If you don't want to get loans and wish to pay for college yourself, you may want to go to a community college for as long as you can. This way you are paying cheap tuition to get all of your general education and miscellaneous subjects out of the way. When you've exhausted every course, transfer to a four year university for the last leg of your college. This will save you thousands of dollars and you end up with the same diploma as if you went all four years to a university.

Dorms

Dorms are expensive, however living in a dorm environment your first year away from home can be a memorable experience. You will make life long memories and friendships with some of your fellow "dormies" since you are all living under one roof, struggling through school and experiencing your new found freedom together. Dorm life is convenient since you get fed and you are on campus so you can roll out of bed and walk to your classes. Living in the dorms can have distractions since the atmosphere is festive in a lot of college dorm facilities. It's easy to get lured to one dorm party after another, so plan your dorm social life wisely. I know this from first hand experience.

If you are lucky enough that your parents will pay for the dorms, or you get some sort of scholarship for living expenses, I highly recommend living in the dorms your first year of school.

Trade School

I'm sure you've seen the commercials where you can earn your paralegal certificate, learn to be a medical assistant or auto mechanic. These are very noble trades and there are private schools that will teach you these trades so you can go right to work.

There are many trade schools offering many courses of study. When I turned 30, I decided to go to broadcasting school to learn how to be a radio DJ. The school cost a few thousand dollars and it lasted about nine months. Trade school typically has contacts with employers in the trades of which they teach and have job placement programs. My husband went to a trade school and learned how to be a refrigeration and air conditioning mechanic. He has since worked in that trade for over 25 years and earns a decent income. The enrollment process in trade school is easy since there are no educational requirements. However, trade schools can be expensive. Don't worry; there are student loan options, grants and other possibilities. Trade schools really want you to attend their school so they will work to get your financing established.

Job Corps

This is a program that was created by the United States Department of Labor. If you are between the ages of 16 and 24 and come from a low income family the Job Corps will train you in many different fields. The best part about Job Corps is that it's absolutely free. Job Corp will teach you how to do jobs such as construction, welding, cooking, dental assisting, truck driving, forestry conservation among many other occupations.

Some Job Corps facilities supply living quarters to students free of charge. My son took advantage of Job Corps right out of high school and learned how to be a glass worker. Job Corps found him a union job right after he finished his courses and he immediately went to work. Check out Job Corps at www.jobcorps.gov

Internship

Another way to learn a trade is to work for free through internship programs. An intern is typically a student that is getting practical training in an actual company. Typically you need to be a college or high school student to enroll in these programs, however some private companies do not have these requirements. Some companies offer on-the-job training programs where you will earn minimum wage and work part time hours. You will need to work another job to pay your bills, but look into internships or on-the-job training programs in companies that interest you. My son took an internship when he was only 16 years old at a graphic arts studio.

Military

This is a subject that I know a lot about. My father is retired from the Army with nine years of his 28 years in service as a Recruiter. My mother and son were also in the Army and I ended up being an Army wife in my early 20s living in Colorado and Germany. As I was never actually in the military myself, I was living in the military world as a family member and learned many things about its ways. Military service is a very important decision, so you must make your decision to enter military service with your eyes wide open.

Recruiters will start calling you during your Junior or Senior year with all sorts of flashy brochures, fliers and videos. The recruiters will make the military look glamorous, exciting and an adventure of a lifetime. They will tell you that all of your education will be paid and will offer you huge enlistment bonuses in the thousands of dollars. Don't be so quick to grab that cash.

I'm not discouraging you from joining the military. I support the military. What I am telling you is that once you take that money, sign the dotted line and head to boot camp you are now owned by the military. There is no quitting, and getting thrown out with a dishonorable discharge will follow you for the rest of your life. You need to do your homework and be extra sure you really want to spend four years following orders and possibly going into a war situation. Let's look at the military in depth.

Military Jobs

Probably the main reason you are considering the military is the instant paycheck, health benefits, room and board, education and possibly free travel to an exotic location. Or, you might have a huge desire to serve your country. That's fantastic! The first thing a recruiter is going to do is help you find a particular job in the military. Be very careful what job you pick. Unlike the rest of the world, you can't quit your job if you decide you don't like the work. Once you are in the military and decide you don't really like the job you are doing, it's very difficult to get reassigned to another job. The military spent time and money training you for the job you initially signed up for.

Before you enlist, the military will have you take a test called the Armed Services Vocational Aptitude Battery (ASVAB) to see what sort of jobs you are best suited for. I took this test when I was 24 and found that I had the aptitude to be a military air traffic controller. Once you take your test, the recruiter will give you a list of jobs (Military Occupation Specialties or MOS) that you qualify for based on your test scores.

IMPORTANT: Don't rely on just the recruiter's opinion or recommendation of a certain job (MOS) that you see on the list. There are some jobs that the military has a hard time filling. Recruiters are instructed to push these jobs onto new recruits. Be very careful if a recruiter tries really hard to get you to take a certain job. This job probably has vacancy issues for a reason!

You will see all sorts of jobs (MOS) on the list. They will have all sorts of lengthy titles. My son's job in the Army was a "Land Combat Electronic Missile Systems Repairer." Wow, that sounds like a job you could take to NASA! The recruiter made it sound very exciting. It turned out to be quite the opposite. Once he got into the job he soon realized he was repairing one small circuit board of a particular piece of equipment. He ended up hating this mundane job. His recruiter told him that he could be an electrician when he got out of the Army. This was not the case. After he was trained on how to fix this type of circuit board, he soon found out that he would only be fixing this piece of equipment in the battlefield. Since he was stationed in the States, he spent his days mopping and sweeping floors. This is common in the military. Since the military is all about war and war activities, when you aren't "at war" you will be doing a lot of mundane work to fill up an eight hour day. My son actually wished he had joined the Infantry so that he could be out "in the field" practicing warfare rather than sweeping the floors and mowing lawns.

As normal as these jobs sound, in the world of the military these jobs could be something completely unique that will only apply in the military. Your job in the military may only be repairing a particular circuit board that is only found on certain piece of war machinery as was my son's case. Jobs that are strictly combat related such as infantry, tank driver, field artillery, etc, are self explanatory. There should be no surprise that you will be running around with a gun or firing a big cannon in the desert. This just might be your thing.

However, there are some military jobs that are pretty straight forward such as cook, military police, medic, nurse and airplane or diesel mechanic. These jobs would most likely transfer to the civilian world. Remember, you are in the military and even though you are only a cook, you can get sent to a dangerous place to flip pancakes!

In the first few days of the Iraq war in 2003, a convoy of cooks, clerks and mechanics fell behind from their group in the middle of the desert of Iraq. They took a wrong turn and found themselves in hostile territory. Many were killed and a few were taken captive by the Iraqi Army. Cook, Shoshana Johnson and File Clerk, Jessica Lynch were severely injured and taken as prisoners of war.

Since these people weren't in combat jobs, they didn't receive the extra combat training that soldiers who were in actual combat jobs did. These cooks, clerks and mechanics only received the minimal combat training they learned in boot camp. I was also told by ex-soldiers that these people probably weren't issued the best weapons since the better weapons were issued to the infantry. Keep all of this in mind if you think you are going to be safe by signing up as a cook or clerk. You are in the military and may be exposed to everything if deployed to a war situation.

My advice is for you to talk to many people who have served or are serving in all branches of the military. Ask them what jobs they have and if they like what they do. If the person is now a civilian, ask that person if they are currently doing their military job as a civilian. Ask many questions.

I don't have anything against recruiters, my dad was a recruiter. However, they are required to sign as many people into the military as they can so they are motivated to not give you the entire picture. They don't lie, they just don't tell you everything.

Remember, the military has one mission and that is to protect and defend the United States using arms.

Every single job in the military, even a cook or clerk is immersed in this mission. Do your own homework before you enlist. It's a long four years if you are completely unhappy with your decision.

The Good News About the Military

If you have done all of your homework and decided what branch of the armed forces, (Army, Air Force, Navy, Marines, National Guard, Coast Guard) you would like to join, congratulations. You are on your way to gallantly serving your country. I hope you also did your homework to find out what job you would be most interested in.

The military can be a great option if you want to see new places, travel overseas, meet people from different parts of the country and different cultures. As a military wife, I enjoyed meeting families from all over the United States and getting to live in Germany was the thrill of a lifetime. When we were stationed in Germany, I made life long friends with the people I met while living there.

You will get full medical benefits, a place to live, food and if you are married you will get basic allowance for quarters to live off base. If you work your way up to Specialist, E-4 or higher, you may qualify for on-base housing for you, your spouse and kids. Most newly enlisted recruits live in the barracks with other recruits.

Other good news – the military can mature you.

Rank

If you have only a high school diploma or GED you will start out at as an enlisted person with a rank of Private (Army/Marines), Seaman (Navy), and Airman (Air Force). You will eventually move up the ladder to E-4 and then to the rank of a non-commissioned officer such as a Sergeant (Army). Sometimes, if you have a year or two of college under your belt, you may be able to enlist as an E-3 or higher. Check with your recruiter on your eligibility. The military is constantly changing the enlistment rules and requirements.

If you enlist in the military with a four year college degree, you could be eligible to go to Officer's Candidate School to become an Officer.

Do yourself a favor, find people who are military savvy and have no agenda and Ask! Ask! Ask!

Benefits of Military Service

If you serve your contractual term in the military you will be eligible for the G.I. Bill ,which can help you pay for college. You may also qualify for some medical services, buy a house with little or no money down and other great benefits.

Once you fulfill your four year enlistment term and you decide the military is the life for you, you now have the title of "lifer." That means you will end up retiring from the military after 20 years or more of service. If you retire from the military, you will get life long health benefits for you and your spouse, a retirement salary, and you will be able to travel anywhere in the world on a military plane for free or next to free. (Note: spouses have certain restrictions on air travel on military flights) Think about it. If you go into the military at the age of 18, you could be retired at 38 years of age! You can retire from the military with full benefits and go on to have a second career if you chose.

Get a Job

If college, trade school or the military are not your thing, then go to work. With little or no job skills right out of high school, your options are limited. You might start working right away in a restaurant. However I've had friends and relatives who started out as waitresses and drive through cashiers who worked their way up to management, making a decent income down the road. However, you will get minimum wage for quite some time until you work your way up.

Maybe you have an idea for your own business when you get out of high school. By all means, go forth. If you can get someone with experience to help you with your business plan and help to get your financing in order, all you need to do is get out there and do it. If you can stand living at home for a couple of years, and your parents don't mind, you will save a lot of money while you are getting your life in order. Don't let the comfort of your nest trap you in a circle of procrastination!

Moving Out

Eventually you will move out and set sail in your own ship. You might get an apartment on your own or you will bunk with other sailors to save on rent money. Which ever you decide, you will need to be prepared for this important decision. It will most likely take about a thousand dollars to move into a decent apartment. Landlords will want first and last months rent, a deposit and a credit check. Since you don't have any credit established, your parents will have to co-sign for your apartment.

You will then have to get your utilities turned on if you want lights, heat and air conditioning which will require some sort of deposit depending on the utility company. Your apartment will be pretty uncomfortable if you don't have a bed or any furniture. This isn't a big deal. You can get really cheap stuff at garage sales. I covered cardboard boxes with cloth and used them as end tables when I was broke and living out on my own. If you have a car, you will have to include the expense of running and insuring your car into the mix of your living on your own expenses. You can save a ton of money if you get a couple of roommates to share expenses. You will love having your own place! I know I do!

Quiz
True or False

A) Learning how your car works could save you money._____

B) Your ATM receipt shows your most current bank balance._____

C) You can easily become overdrawn in your bank account._____

D) A judge is the only person who can grant an emancipation._____

E) You must pick a major right away if you plan on attending college._____

F) Job Corps is a free job training program._____

Fill In the Blanks

G) College scholarships are_____

H) If you sign up to be a cook in the military, you might be_____in the desert.

I) Military benefits include_____

J) If you get your own apartment you may have to get a _____ to save on expenses.

Extra Credit: How have you planned for the day when you leave home? (When you get the boot)

_____
_____
_____
_____

Set Sail

Congratulations Cadet Sailor, you have now been promoted to Captain. If you got through this manual and took it to heart, you have earned your Captain's stripes and are fully prepared to launch your ship. As you plan to set sail in your newly crafted ship, remember that you must still plan for each and every trip that lies ahead. Every Captain has to look at their maps and plan their course before they set sail into uncharted waters.

While you are still in your planning mode and maybe not quite ready to set sail just yet, let me give you some helpful tips to keep you focused and on track for the trip ahead.

Get the best grades you can in school. You now have all of the tools to be a better learner and how to deal with your teachers.

Have respect for yourself and others. Take good care of your body, it's the only one you have. Give your parents some slack, they are stuck with you too!

When things are going wrong, shout out an S.O.S. Don't keep the junk bottled up inside to rot and fester. Let your feelings be known and work to help yourself.

Plan your course wisely. In your Junior year, you should be thinking about your next three years. Start the planning process now using all of the tools in this manual.

Create your own Captain's Club. I know it sounds nerdy and you don't have to call it by that name but get yourself surrounded by a group of friends who want to make a group effort in building your boats. Figure out together how you are going to handle getting the boot.
It's not too early to network and meet people who can help you make some very important decisions. You might have a friend whose sister is in the Navy. That would be a valuable connection of you are thinking of joining. You have to start asking questions to get the answers.

Set your Goals

Make a list of the things you want to accomplish one week at a time. Start out small. Maybe your goal is to get a good grade on a particular project. Plan out your week with your calendar you created and plan each hour of each day for the next week. You will be surprised of the results when you make yourself stick to a schedule. You can even plan some fun time in that schedule. However, you must stick to the schedule. If you ended up with a good grade on your project, you have completed your goal. Congratulations!

Here is a list to get you started on a goal:
A) What do I want to do (goal)?
B) What do I want to learn or know?
C) What resources can help me get to my goal?
D) Keep a calendar and stick to it.

Finally

Don't rule out your teachers and parents. These people actually lived a whole lifetime of experiences. They know a lot of stuff. Really they do! **Just ask them!**

Bon Voyage Captain!

Try to stay out of the rocks!

Quiz Answer Key

Quiz Page 28:

(A - T), (B - F), (C - F), (D - T), (E - F)

(F - You think that you don't need guidance), (G - Drama, Sad, Victim of abuse) (H - Clean room, Go to school, Have respect for others) (I - Dyslexia, ADHD, OCD) (J - To learn)

Quiz Page 42:

(A - T), (B - T), (C - T), (D - T)

(E - Telling them I love the subject they teach), (F - Act out parts of history in costume), (G - Take an interest in their life as a person, Make friends)

Quiz Page 53

(A - T), (B - T), (C - T), (D - T), (E - F), (F - T)

(G - Trained), (H - Personality), (I - Self discipline), (J - Time)

Quiz Page 61

(A - T), (B - T), (C - T), (D - T), (E - T), (F - T)

(G - Football field), (H - Speeding driver), (I - Passengers), (J - The other driver was following traffic laws), (K- Distracted or on drugs/alcohol)

Quiz Page 77:

(A - T), (B - T), (C - T), (D - F), (E - T), (F - T), (G - T)

(H - Talk to your doctor), (I - Talk to your doctor),
(J - Computer enhanced), (K - Year)

Quiz Page 106

(A - T), (B - F), (C - T), (D - T), (E - F), (F - T)

(G - Funds given to students by organizations or individuals),
(H - Flipping pancakes), (I - Housing and medical benefits),
(J - Roommate)

Acknowledgements

My husband Alex for putting up with my long hours at my laptop * William Gutierrez for painstakingly editing my work * Barbara Keck (Lesley Suthard's mom)

Thank You!

www.ingramcontent.com/pod-product-compliance
Lightning Source LLC
Chambersburg PA
CBHW032129090426
42743CB00007B/520